Nebraska Fish Species

Game Fish & Panfish

Billy Grinslott & Kinsey Marie Books

ISBN - 9781965098998

Orange spotted sunfish are mostly found in floodplains of the United States or shallow mucky ponds. Its beautiful shiny silvery-blue body has reddish-orange spots, which give it its name, orange spotted sunfish. They are usually too small to be popular with anglers. Their average length is 3 inches. They are a small fish.

The Green Sunfish is blue green in color. It has yellow flecks on both its scales and some parts of its sides. The Green Sunfish also has broken blue stripes which is why some people confuse it with the Bluegill. Green Sunfish are very adaptable, they can live in any body of water that has vegetation or weeds. Green sunfish are opportunistic feeders, consuming insects, small fish, and other invertebrates.

Redear sunfish are known for their red or orange-edged gill flaps. They are a type of sunfish that thrive in warm, quiet waters, feeding primarily on mollusks and snails, and can grow up to 12 inches and weigh as much as 2 pounds. They are also known as shellcracker, due to their diet and the way they crush shells. The redear sunfish will thrive in most warm-water lakes and streams.

Redhorse fishes are part of the sucker family and are known for their bottom-facing mouths and fleshy lips which they use to suck food off the bottom. Redhorse has large, molar-like throat teeth that are an adaptation for crushing the shells of mollusks. redhorses construct nests in clean gravel, using their tails to sweep and their mouths to carry rocks or move materials with their heads.

The Rock Bass is not actually a bass but a member of the sunfish family. The biggest Rock Bass ever caught on record weighs about three pounds and was a little over one foot long. Rock bass prefer waters with rocky vegetated areas, that's how they got their name.

The Pumpkinseed is also known as pond perch, sun perch, and punky's sunfish. It can be found in numerous lakes, ponds, and rivers. It is their body shape resembling the seed of a pumpkin, that inspired their name. Pumpkinseed sunfish have speckles on their orangish colored sides and back, with a yellow to orange belly and chest. They are active during the day and rest at night near the bottom or in shelter areas.

The bluegill also considered a sunfish is the most popular fish to fish for. They are called pan fish because they are about the size of a frying pan. Bluegills love to eat insects and bugs. They have good vision and rely on their keen eyesight to feed. Three types in this group are the Bluegill, Sunfish, and Pumpkinseed.

The two most famous perches are the common perch and the yellow perch. The yellow perch has a brilliant greenish yellow color with orange fins. The yellow perch is the biggest one and can grow to a size of 18 inches. It's also known as the jumbo perch. The other type of perch is the white perch.

There are two main types of crappies. The white crappie and the black crappie. They are also members of the sunfish family. The difference between the white and black crappie is one has dark spots and the other has dark lines and is lighter in color. The white crappie has six dorsal fin spines, whereas the black crappie has eight dorsal fin spines. The white crappie can grow bigger and more of the bigger white crappie are caught in North America. The largest crappie caught in Nebraska weighs 4 pounds and 8 ounces.

The sucker fish has the same mouth as a carp. They got their name because their mouth is like a suction cup. They normally are bottom feeders and suck their food from the bottom of the lake. Many people use sucker fish to fish for northern pike and other big game fish. The largest sucker fish (specifically a Blue Sucker) caught in Nebraska weighed 18 lbs. 14 oz. It was caught in the Missouri River.

Flathead Catfish, their body is wide but flattened and very low in height. Both eyes are on the top of the flattened head, giving excellent vision to see upward. Flathead catfish live mainly in large bodies of water like big rivers and reservoirs. They prefer deep pools. The largest flathead catfish caught in Nebraska weighed 89 pounds. The fish was 53.5 inches long.

The black bullhead and yellow bullhead are part of the catfish family. They usually only grow to about 10 inches long. They use their whiskers to help find food. The bullhead is the most common member of the catfish family. Bullheads live in the water containing low oxygen levels. They can survive on low oxygen areas, where other fish can't.

There are several species of catfish. The Channel Catfish are the most fished catfish species with around 8 million anglers fishing for them per year. Blue catfish are known for their size, reaching over 100 pounds. Blue catfish, like other catfish, lack scales and have smooth skin. They have barbels (whiskers) around their mouths, which are used for sensing and tasting food. They are generally slate blue on the back and silvery/white on the underside The largest blue catfish caught in Nebraska weighed 100 pounds, 8 ounces.

Bowfins can breathe both air and water, putting them at an advantage in low-oxygen waters. Bowfins are often described as prehistoric relics. This is because species can be traced to fossils from the Cretaceous, Eocene and Jurassic period. The largest Bowfin caught in Nebraska weighed 8 pounds.

White Bass range in color from a silvery white to a pale green. Their backs are mostly black, while their sides and belly are pale with stripes running along them. White Bass are related to Striped Bass and called wipers. The largest White Bass caught in Nebraska weighed 5 pounds.

Striped bass are often called Stripers. Striped bass live in both salt and fresh water. Striped bass have very sensitive eyes and will seek deep water when the sun is out. Striped bass have a preferred water temperature range of from 55° F to 68° F, and swim to find water of these temperatures. Striped bass can grow up to 5 feet long and weigh up to 77 pounds. The largest recorded striped bass was 125 pounds and was caught in 1891. The largest striped bass caught in Nebraska weighed 64 pounds and 15 ounces.

Yellow bass, scientifically known as Morone mississippiensis, are a relatively small, schooling fish with a golden-yellow body and dark stripes, often found in rivers and lakes, particularly in areas with dense vegetation. The average size for this fish is 12 inches in length and one pound in weight. They are also known as rockfish, streaker, and yellow belly. The largest Yellow bass caught in Nebraska weighed 1 pound 9 ounces.

Wipers are a hybrid striped bass, also known as a wiper or Whiterock bass. It is a hybrid between the striped bass and the white bass. Hybrids closely resemble both striped bass and white bass making identification difficult, particularly for young fish. Either way, you get a fish that has both genetics of the striped and white bass. The largest wiper bass caught in Nebraska weighed 21 pounds and 9 ounces.

The burbot, also known as the eel pout. They get their name because they have a serpent-like or eel-like body. They can wrap their tail around things. There's nothing to worry about if you catch one, they may try to wrap their tail around your arm, but they are harmless. Burbots are adapted to cold water and are found in large, cold rivers, lakes, and reservoirs, primarily preferring freshwater habitats. Burbots are also known as eelpout, lingcod, and lawyer. The largest burbot caught in Nebraska weighed 6 lbs. 9 oz.

There are few different species of Gar, the Longnose gar, Short nose and spotted gar. The Gar got its name because of its long mouth that looks like an alligator's mouth. The alligator gar is one of the biggest freshwater fish growing up to 10 feet long. The world record for a catch was set at 327 pounds. The largest gar caught in Nebraska was a longnose gar weighing 24 pounds 14 ounces, it was 57 inches long.

Sturgeons have sharp spines on their back, so be careful when handling them. Instead of scales, sturgeon skin is covered in bony plates called scutes, which can be very sharp on young sturgeon. Sturgeons have been around since the dinosaur days. Sturgeons mostly live in large, freshwater lakes and rivers. Their average lifespan is 50 to 60 years. The largest lake sturgeon caught in Nebraska was a 212.2-pound fish, 84.2 inches long.

Male freshwater drum make a rumbling or grunting sound by contracting muscles along their air bladder walls. They have large, ivory-like ear bones that can be up to an inch in diameter, which Native Americans used as necklaces or bracelets and sometimes referred to as the lucky stones. Freshwater drum are primarily bottom feeders, spending much of their time near the bottom of lakes and rivers in search of food. The largest freshwater drum caught in Nebraska weighed 29 pounds and 6 ounces.

Buffalo Fish are sometimes confused with carp. Buffalo fish have a downward-facing mouth, capable of sucking bits of food out of the silt and sand on the bottom. They have broad bodies, blunt heads, and silvery gray or brown scales. Buffalo fish are members of the suckerfish family. The largest bigmouth buffalo caught in Nebraska weighed 64 pounds.

Carp have long been an important food fish to humans. Carp are bottom feeders for the most part and their mouth is made like a suction cup, so they can suck food off the bottom. Carp are good for a lake because they help clean the bottom of the lake. The largest carp caught in Nebraska is a common carp that weighed 39 pounds and 8 ounces.

The rainbow trout gets its name because of its brilliant colors. Rainbow trout populations are good indicators of water pollution because they can only survive in clean waters. They like to live in rivers and streams. Rainbow trout rank among the top five most sought game fish in North America. The largest rainbow trout caught in Nebraska weighed 14 pounds and 2 ounces. It was 29.5 inches long.

Brown trout can live up to 20 years. Brown trout have higher tolerance for warmer waters than either brook or rainbow trout. Brown trout can be found on almost every continent except Antarctica, and many can be found living in the ocean. The largest Brown trout caught in Nebraska weighed 20 pounds and 1 ounce.

Brook trout are characterized by their olive-green bodies with pale, worm-like markings, red spots with bluish halos, and orange-red fins with white and black edges. They can grow up to 12 inches in length. Brook trout are cold-water fish that prefer clean, clear, and cold streams, lakes, and ponds. The largest brook trout caught in Nebraska weighed 5 pounds, 1 ounce.

Paddlefish are among the oldest surviving fish species in North America, dating back to about 125 million years ago. Their most distinctive feature is their long, flat, paddle-shaped snout, which helps them detect and locate tiny aquatic animals. The largest paddlefish ever caught in Nebraska was a 113-pound, 4-ounce fish, it was 49.75-inches.

Goldeye fish typically average around 12 inches in length and weigh about 1 pound but can grow up to 20 inches long. Their most distinctive feature is their yellow or gold-colored eyes. Their yellow or gold-colored eyes are adapted for low-light conditions and allows them to see when the water is darker. Goldeye are also known as mooneye. The largest Goldeye fish caught in Nebraska weighed 3 pounds and 15.5 ounces.

Spotted bass have rows of dark spots on their sides and a green pattern along their back. They are also known as Kentucky's or redeye bass. They are a popular and often mistaken for largemouth bass, but they have subtle differences like a smaller mouth. They are known for their aggressive nature and tendency to school together. They prefer rocky bottoms and being in deeper water compared to other bass who like shallow water. The largest Spotted bass caught in Nebraska weighed 3 pounds, 12 ounces, was 18.25 inches long.

The largemouth bass is the most sought-after bass in North America. Largemouth bass live in just about every lake in North America. They have great hearing and can hear a crayfish crawling on the bottom of the lake. The largest largemouth bass caught in Nebraska weighed 10 pounds and 11 ounces.

Smallmouth bass have a smaller mouth than the largemouth bass. They also have different markings and are lighter in color. They don't live in most lakes because they prefer living in colder water. They are typically found in the northern states in America because the water is cooler. The current world record smallmouth is an 11-pound, 15-ounce fish caught in Dale Hollow Lake. The largest Smallmouth Bass caught in Nebraska was a 7-pound, 4-ounce fish, measured at 22 inches.

The sauger is part of the walleye family. There are 2 different types of saugers. The normal sauger and the suageye. The saugeye is a mix of the sauger and walleye. The suageye have white eyes just like the walleye. The sauger and suageye are smaller than the walleye. Saugers are more likely to be found in large rivers with deep pools but are also found in lakes. The largest sauger ever caught in Nebraska weighed 8 pounds and 5 ounces.

The walleye got its name because of its white looking eyes. Their eyes collect light, even in low light conditions. This means they can see in the dark. Because they can see in the dark, they mostly feed at night. During the daytime their eyes are very sensitive, so they usually head for deeper water or shady places. Walleye like to live in cooler water and are normally found in the upper part of North America. The largest walleye caught in Nebraska was a 16-pound, 2-ounce fish, it was 33 inches long.

Pickerel kind of look like northern pike, but they are not. The Pike is larger in size than the Pickerel. The Pickerel has more spots than the Pike, but the Pike has spots on its fins and pickerel don't. Pickerel has a dark bar beneath their eyes and northern pike don't. Pickerel are also known as gunfish or slime darts. The largest Chain Pickerel caught in Nebraska weighed 3.5 pounds and was 25 1/2 inches long.

The Northern Pike is one of the most sought-after fish for anglers. It got its name because it likes to live in cooler water mainly in the northern states of North America. The northern pike is a very aggressive predator. They don't like to live in groups with other fish, they are very territorial and like to live alone. Their behavior is closely affected by weather conditions. The largest Northern Pike caught in Nebraska weighed 30 lbs. 1 oz. Was 47 inches long.

The muskellunge called the Musky or Muskie for short is one of the biggest game fish in freshwater lakes. The largest on record was 69 pounds, 15 ounces. The Muskie likes to live in cooler water and can be found in most lakes in the upper part of north America. Anglers look at Muskellunges as trophy fish. They are hard to catch, there's a saying that it takes a thousand casts to catch one. The largest muskellunge caught in Nebraska weighed 41 lbs. and 8 oz and was 52 inches long.

Fun Facts About Nebraska Fish

1 - Channel Catfish is the official state fish of Nebraska and is found in nearly many bodies of water in the state.

2 - The largest fish ever caught in Nebraska was a paddlefish weighing 113 pounds, 4 ounces.

3 - Nebraska is home to over 100 fish species, with 78 considered to be native.

4 - The state has records for various fish, like the blue cat 100 lbs. 8 oz. channel catfish 31 lbs. 13 oz. flathead catfish 89 lbs.

5 - The most frequently caught fish in Nebraska is arguably the sunfish, particularly the bluegill.

6 – A record goldfish was caught in Nebraska. It weighed 6 pounds and 12 ounces.

7 - Smelling and tasting. Fish use their nostrils to smell, and catfish use their barbels or whiskers to taste.

Author Page

Billy Grinslott & Kinsey Marie Books

ISBN – 9781965098998

Thanks

www.ingramcontent.com/pod-product-compliance
Lightning Source LLC
Chambersburg PA
CBHW060851270326
41934CB00002B/97